52

Simple Ways to Live Green

Easy Things That Help Save Our Planet

Terri Paajanen

Terri Paajanen, Author
Copyright © 2014 by **Mango Media, Inc.**

Cover Design: Elina Diaz
Infographics Designed by Roberto Núñez
Interior Layout: Elina Diaz, Maria Llorens, Cristian Velecico and Hugo
Villabona
Interior Images: RetroClipArt/Shutterstock.com

Mango Media
MIAMI
info@mangomedia.us

Publisher's Note: This is a work of nonfiction. The author has researched and recreated some, not all, of the vignettes and/or methods that are described within the text. In some instances the author or editor has changed or removed certain elements that may or may not have pertained to the efficiency of the vignette and/or method. They may have changed some identifying characteristics and details such as physical properties, occupations and/or places. The efficiency and impact of the vignette and/or method is determined solely by the accuracy of the participation, and Mango Media, Inc., in no way guarantees that they will be executed to perfection.

52 SIMPLE WAYS TO LIVE GREEN Easy Things that Help Save our Planet.
Terri Paajanen -. -- 2nd Ed.
ISBN: 978-1-63353-024-9

"One of the deep secrets of life is that all that is really worth the doing is what we do for others."

— Lewis Carroll

Contents

Level 5: Captain Planet

Level ①

Green Rookie

Waste Less Food

Waste Less Food

Whether it's leftovers from a meal or spoiled food from the fridge, you're probably trashing more food than you should. People tend to ignore food waste because it is organic and easily broken down in nature.

Plan Ahead

The best way to eliminate wasted food is to plan your meals before you cook and shop. Knowing what meals are coming up means that you'll only be buying what you need. It also helps with all those forgotten items that you've bought but never got around to using.

Watch the Expiration Dates

Those silly dates on our food are the cause of a great deal of waste because people toss perfectly fine products just because of the date. Within reason, those dates are just guides. Most food products are good for many days if not weeks longer. Keep an eye on the dates, and plan to use food that is expiring soon.

Use Your Freezer

If you are getting worried that something in your fridge may not get used in time, it might be smarter to toss it in the freezer before it's too late. Meats and many vegetables can be frozen for several months.

Don't Shun Leftovers

Leftover food shouldn't be tossed or ignored until it's no good. Make it part of your routine to serve leftovers during the week or use them in other dishes. Leftover vegetables or pasta can be added to soup, and leftover meats can jazz up a stir fry. Get creative and you'll save money and trash at dinnertime.

 Fact

Americans generally **waste** about **40%** of purchased food.

Buy in Bulk

Now, this tip is about buying bulk foods (the kind where you bag your own) and not just buying large quantities at Costco. Most people know this can be a way to save money with grocery staples like sugar, flour or beans, but there is a great environmental aspect to bulk food too. It's all about the packaging or, really, the lack of packaging.

The specifics vary by the type of food. Some foods are already sold in recyclable packages anyway, so the bigger benefit lies in products that are sold in non-recyclable materials. Things that come in foil-based packages, some types of paper packaging, or all those types of plastic you can't put in your blue bin are examples where bulk is better.

Using non-packaged bulk food in your home can save thousands of pounds of garbage each year. Another benefit to buying food at a bulk store is that you can control your quantities better, which can mean less waste if you only need a small amount. Why buy a package that has more than you need?

1 If you haven't spent any time in a bulk food store recently, the variety of foods available is surprising. Larger stores will carry all your usual baking ingredients, as well as bins of dried fruit, pet food, pasta, candy, coffee, spices, trail mixes, dry cereal, and a lot more. Really good bulk food chains are also carrying plenty of organic options.

2 Get a collection of containers to keep your bulk goodies in. The bags you get at the store are fine for some things, but a sturdier tub or jar would be better for most stuff. Save your old spaghetti sauce or peanut butter jars for free containers.

3 Start shopping at your bulk store next time you need a few things, and see how much money and garbage you can save.

Fact

if all Americans bought just coffee from a bulk bin, it would save **20 million pounds** **OF** foil packaging from the landfill each month.

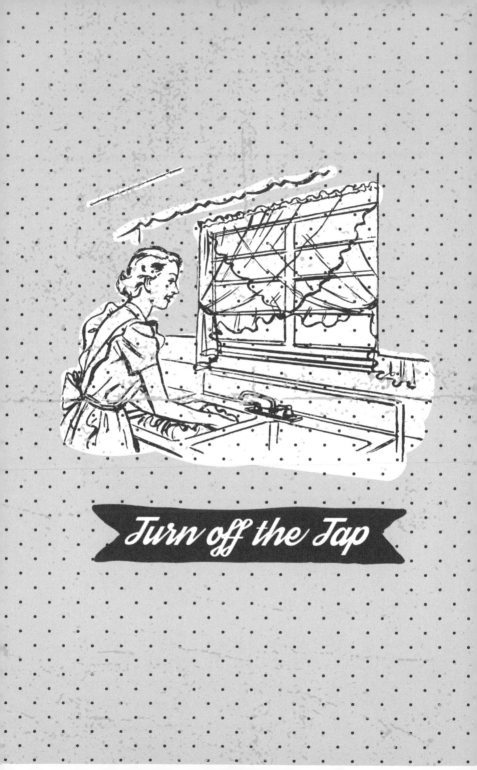

Turn off the Tap

Turn off the Tap

Turn off your tap when you're not actually using it. Most people let it run for several reasons, and every one equals a sizable waste in water.

The biggest culprit is running water while you brush your teeth. Just shut off the water while you scrub your teeth. It's a very simple tip that won't disrupt your life though it may seem awkward at first to keep turning the tap on and off as you rinse off your brush. You'll get the hang of it.

That's not the only time people tend to let the faucet flow. Are you letting the water run to get it nice and cold for a drink? Keep a jug of tap water in the fridge instead, so you can get a cold glass of water without the waste. It's quicker, too.

If you wash your dishes by hand, running the tap until the water is hot is another problem. Depending on how quickly your water heats up, you can waste up to a gallon each time you run it. Since you can't easily keep hot water sitting around for instant use, you have to keep the water from being wasted.

Keep a jug near the sink, and when you run the tap for hot water, just hold on to the water. Then use that supply next time you need water.

And while we're talking about running taps, you should take care not to let any dripping ones go untended. A dripping faucet can waste hundreds (if not thousands) of gallons every year. A wrench and a new washer is probably all you need to green up your taps.

One last tip: if you tend to run a lot of water when rinsing things off, add an aerator to your faucet. You'll get more spray but use less water. They're easy to install, and typically just screw on to the end of your faucet.

Fact

Depending on the water pressure in your home, you can be letting **1 to 2 gallons** of water disappear down the drain **every minute** that tap runs. That's more than **1,500 gallons** of water **wasted each year.**

Improve Your Showers

Improve Your Showers

This might not be the most appealing tip on Monday morning, but cutting back on your shower time can help save water. Quite a bit of water, actually.

You are likely using around 2 1/2 gallons of water for every minute you are in the shower. If you want to save water, time your showers. If you shorten your shower by 2 minutes, that adds up to about 150 gallons of water saved each month. Shaving off just a minute or two will make a difference.

The main environmental savings is reduced water usage, but don't forget that you will also use less hot water which means less wasted power.

Shorter showers aren't your only option. A low-flow shower head can help you cut back on the gallons without actually getting less shower time. The average model will reduce your water consumption to around 1 1/2 gallons per minute. They're not that expensive and just screw on in place of the old head. You won't even need a plumber.

You might try showering a little less often as well. The cultural norm in North America is to shower daily. That's 25 gallons of water gone each day. Maybe you can change your thinking a bit and cut that down. Unless you a doing a lot of physical (i.e sweaty) labor, most people can stay perfectly clean with an every-other-day shower.

Any combination of these ideas will improve the environmental impact of your shower, and save hundreds (if not thousands) of gallons of water in the process.

Fact

You are likely using around **2½ gallons** of water for every minute you are the shower.

With a typical shower of **10 minutes**, that's more than **25 gallons** every time (possibly every single day).

Turn Off the Computer at Night

Older folks in the 1990s will remember hearing the standard tip that you should leave your computer running through the night. The problem was that the powering up sequence would surge a large amount of energy through the components, actually causing more wear and tear on your computer.

Today, that no longer applies. Computers use more power if they sit idle all night instead (even when asleep or on standby). Aside from the financial losses, that wasted power can equal about 20 million tons of carbon dioxide emissions to produce all that electricity.

It really only takes a moment to properly shut down and turn off your computer each night, and it's easy enough to make it a usual habit. Not only will you use less power, you will extend the life of your computer. It needs the chance to cool down. If you do need to leave it running because it's doing something necessary, turn off the monitor.

There is one instance when letting your computer run at night may be the wiser choice, and that is when you have to run a particularly long process (like a big backup, download, or virus scan). If you live in an area that has electricity charges based on the time of day, it will cost you less to do these things at night.

Fact

According to a PC Energy Report, workers in the USA waste nearly **$3 billion** in power costs each year.

Books

Try the Library

Try the Library

Don't roll your eyes at this tip just yet. The library may not be as relevant in this cyber age of paper-less Kindle books, but that doesn't mean it doesn't have a place in an eco-enthusiast's life.

Granted, switching your book choices to digital ebooks is a fantastic way of reducing paper consumption and waste, there is still room for the benefits of a library.

For one thing, the books are free. Though it is possible to populate your ebook reader with free books, it's not always that easy. If you enjoy reading the latest novels, you'll almost always have to pay for them. On the other hand, they're always free at the library. And generally, just having the feel of a physical book in your hands is enough of a reason to stick with "real" books.

How many books are we talking about here? Billions. Even with recycled content, that's a lot of trees. Getting books from the library means fewer new books need to be created.

Your library may have DVDs or even board games available. Some have other tools available that might come in handy, like computers and access to research databases. A library with a busy genealogy community might have a subscription to Ancestry.com, for example.

If you get stuck because you can't find that certain book, don't hesitate to ask about it. Most books can be transferred between libraries at no cost to you, which can give you indirect access to larger collections without having to go anywhere.

And one more jab at ebooks: Though the idea of paper-less books may seem like the perfect green solution, there is more to it than that. These devices are creating demand for more plastic and electronic components (like metal toxins). Out-of-date devices are creating more hazardous waste each year. They may save paper, but at what cost?

Fact

Well, there are nearly **one hundred thousand** new titles published each year in the United States, and there are **several billion** books sold every year.  That equals more than **30 million** trees cut down to make the paper.

Download Your Software

These days, it's a very common option to just download a copy of newly purchased software. Not only is it quicker, it's the environmentally savvy choice too. Having a CD and accompanying paperwork mailed to you isn't really necessary and just creates more trash. This goes for music as well. A digital download is about as clean as you can get.

In the past 10 years, downloading has saved more than 23 million tons of greenhouse gas emissions (partly from all the delivery and partly from the production of CDs or cassettes). CD cases are made from a particularly hard form of plastic, and they are seldom accepted for recycling. That means they go straight into the garbage once they're no longer needed.

If you are concerned about the accidental deletion of your software once you've downloaded it, you can save an extra copy of the download file on your hard drive or other storage device. It's a little added security without having to actually have a CD shipped to you. If you keep your order information, many companies will let you re-download later if you need to.

 Fact

Globally, the practice of downloading music instead of buying CDs has **saved** approximately **6.5 billion miles** of driving every year.

Use Reusable Shopping Bags

Use Reusable Shopping Bags

This is probably the oldest green tip around, yet it remains one of the best. Stop accepting plastic shopping bags every time you go to the store. You'll reduce the demand and the harmful effects of plastic simply by bringing your own.

Have a supply of sturdy reusable bags in your home, and train yourself to bring two with you everywhere you go. If you only carry them when you plan on making a purchase, you won't develop that rock-solid habit. Keep a few in the car, too.

They're not only for big purchases like groceries. Heavy tote-style bags are versatile because they can carry just about anything. A lightweight nylon bag can be tucked in a pocket or purse for when you need something small. If it's with you, you'll remember to use it.

Try carrying your purchases without a bag. We tend to feel naked carrying something out of the store without a bag, but it shouldn't be a receipt. If you don't need one, don't take one.

If you do slip up, make sure to recycle your plastic bags. Put them all in a single bag and drop them in your recycling bin. Many grocery stores now accept them as well.

Plastic bags can be harmful outside of the landfill, too. They can end up in local ecosystems as free-flying litter. Once they start to shred apart, animals get tangled in the plastic or choke on the pieces. They seem flimsy, but they are a huge environmental problem.

Overall, the United States consumes enough plastic bags to use up 12 million barrels of oil. Not only are plastic bags creating a lot of garbage, they are using up precious resources while they're at it. Say "no" to a bag next time you shop.

A plastic grocery bag will linger around in a landfill **for centuries** (some studies say 1,000 years).

Get to Know the
Farmer's Market

Get to Know the Farmer's Market

Browsing the local farmer's market isn't just a pleasant way to spend a Saturday afternoon. You should make it an expedition to find a lovely mix of healthy and ecologically-minded food. Of course, not every vendor will have a green cornucopia laid out for you, but it's a better offering than the commercially-farmed produce at the supermarket.

Remember that even small farmers may use pesticides, so don't assume everything is organic. But smaller operations do tend to be more natural. There shouldn't be any GMO worries, and home-grown produce isn't going to be waxed or dyed. Talk with vendors and see who's farming in a way you support.

The biggest benefit from shopping at the farmer's market isn't the food itself, but the fact that everything has been grown in the area. You won't contribute to thousands of miles of truck exhaust and fuel consumption by buying an apple that travelled across the continent. The term "localvore" has been coined for people who model their diet around what is available near them, and it's becoming a growing trend.

Buying from local farms means less support for big commercial farms, which helps reduce the damage these huge agribusinesses do to the environment. Their intensive methods ruin the soil and the chemical run-off ruins the water. Smaller farms are a better choice.

If you can't get to a market, see if nearby farms offer delivery or pick-up. You can subscribe to get a big box of fresh produce each week based on what's in season. Check out CSAs (community-sponsored agriculture) in your area for more options.

You might even save some money. Folks selling at a market don't have the same overhead as a big supermarket, and you can often see that in their prices. Naturally grown foods are better for you—and better for the Earth.

Fact

The average piece of produce travels **1,300 miles** from where it was grown to your **supermarket**, particularly when you buy food that isn't in **season** where you live.

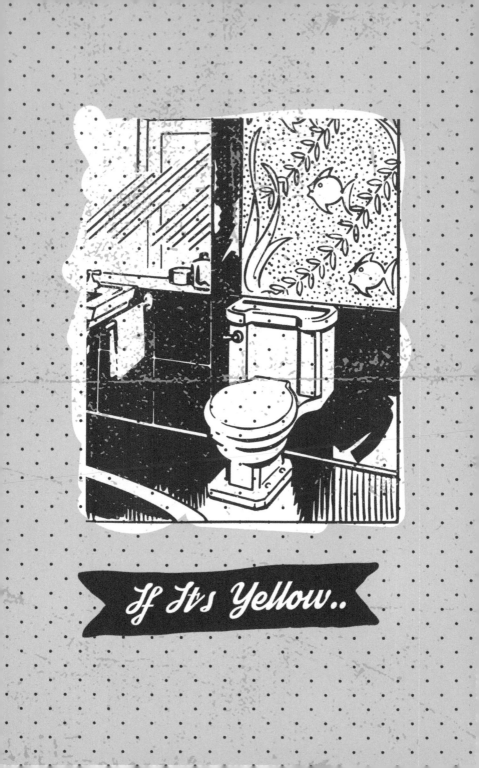

If It's Yellow..

If It's Yellow...

Hopefully this tip won't offend anyone's delicate sensibilities, but with so much water usage going on in the bathroom, it should be discussed. We're talking about the old saying, "If it's yellow, let it mellow. If it's brown, flush it down." Many eco-enthusiasts are changing their flushing habits to save water.

If the lovely poem hasn't made it clear, the idea is that you don't flush the toilet after every use (when it's yellow, in particular). The concept might seem peculiar to some, but there are some parts of the world where this is pretty much standard procedure.

Every time you flush, you are using anywhere from 1 to 2 gallons of water. That's actually a lot of water when you just need to get rid of a few ounces of urine. You can save quite a bit of water and money by flushing only when necessary.

With fresh water becoming an important commodity, this can be a valuable tip. Don't dismiss it out of hand just because it sounds a little icky. The smell from a single unflushed use is generally not that noticeable if you keep the lid down. Cleaning chores may increase as the bowl will get dirty faster between flushes. If you already clean once a week, you won't need to more than that.

For the ladies in the house, there is the issue of toilet paper build-up with each use. If you're not flushing, the paper will start to accumulate. The most common practice is to have a good-sized trash can (with a lid) in the bathroom and drop the wet paper in there rather than in the bowl. It's not necessary if you don't like the idea. A little mellowing through the day is going to save water, regardless.

Fact

if you held off on flushing just **3 times** over the course **of the day** you would save nearly **5 gallons** of **water**.

A year of following this routine would save more than **1,600** gallons of **water**, per person.

Air Dry Your Clothes

Air Dry Your Clothes

Don't skip this tip if you live in the city or a neat little suburb. Clotheslines aren't just for rural farmhouses anymore. Not only can you commune with nature as you hang your clothes, you can help the Earth by reducing your electricity consumption.

Your clothes dryer is one of the biggest power users in the home, and using it less often will definitely have an impact (yes, even if you have a very energy-efficient model).

A couple loads a week will add up quickly. Every load you don't dry indoors is going to mean less pollution in our environment. Frequent dryer usage adds hundreds of pounds of carbon to the air over the year.

In fact, you could probably measure your carbon savings in tons, rather than pounds, if you completely switch to air drying.

Thankfully, drying your clothes out on a clothesline is cheap and easy. There may be an initial investment to buy a length of line and a set of pulleys, but that's it. Large home improvement stores should have convenient starter kits.

Not enough space in your yard (or no yard at all)? Don't let that stand in your way. You can get a small free-standing rack, and they hold a lot of clothes for their size. An umbrella-style rack is another option for a small yard. If you have no outside space at all, then you can let your clothes air-dry inside. It just takes longer.

A warm day with little or no wind is best for drying clothes outside. A very windy or rainy day is obviously not ideal.

Remember it doesn't have to be all or nothing. If you only reduce your dryer time by 3 or 4 loads each month, it's going to make a difference. Not only will you be polluting less, but your utility bill will also get lighter.

> **Fact**
>
> On average, each load of clothes that you dry with an electric dryer will add **4 1/2 pounds of carbon** to the atmosphere.

Full Loads Only

Modern washing machines and dishwashers are a wonderful convenience, but they aren't great when it comes to water consumption.

With both, you want to maximize your water usage every time you get the machine running. Even if you are running a very efficient machine, you want to get the most out of each cycle.

Make the best use of that water and get every possible dish that you can in your dishwasher. Don't get into the habit of running it after each meal simply to get things cleaned up. If you only have a few items and really need them washed, wash them by hand.

The same story goes for the washing machine. Your favorite pair of pants is dirty and you just toss them into the machine without thinking about it. Make the hard sacrifice of wearing another pair until you have enough clothes to make up a load, and only do the washing then. Even if you turn the dial down to the lowest water level, you still will waste water if you are just washing one or two items.

The "small load" settings are very helpful but overall you'll get the best efficiency for your water use by running a full-sized load. How much water your washer will use depends on the model. The older top-loaders can use around 40 gallons per load, and a front-loader will be around half that.

On the other hand, don't get too zealous cramming every piece of fabric you own into the washing machine for a single load. You'll likely overwork the machine and your clothes won't get clean.

How much water your washer will use depends on the model. A front-loader will use half as a much water as a top-loader. That might be another thing to consider when you are in the market for new appliances.

> **Fact**

A typical dishwasher will use between 5 and **6 gallons** of water per load, no matter how full it is.

WET WASH

Avoid Dry Cleaning

Avoid Dry Cleaning

Anyone with a business wardrobe is probably familiar with dry cleaning, and it shouldn't be a complete surprise that it's not a very environmentally friendly practice.

If you don't know how it works, it is only called "dry" because it is a process that doesn't use water. It uses liquid chemical solvents instead. The main ingredient for most dry cleaners is perchloroethylene (known simply as "perc"). It's a highly toxic substance that causes a long list of health issues (dizziness, headaches, eye and nose irritation, respiratory damage) and has been linked with cancer.

Most of the solvent is removed before you get your clothes back, but there is always some level of residue that can get on your skin. The problem is the pollution created in the cleaner's shop rather than the clothes you bring home. The perc fumes can get in the air, and leaks or spillage around the equipment can mean perc works its way into the soil and groundwater.

Don't want to support this kind of pollution? Build your wardrobe around clothes that don't need to be dry cleaned in the first place. Delicate items can be hand-washed with gentle soap and laid out flat to dry. This would be the case for most cotton, linen, polyester or even cashmere.

Silk, wool or velvet are probably still going to need the professional touch. Minimize your perc exposure by only cleaning those items when they need it, not just after one use. But the best idea is to stop buying "dry-clean only" clothes.

A new process called "wet cleaning" is coming about these days that does use water instead of the harsh solvents, which makes it a much greener choice. If you see a shop offering it in your area, give it a try.

Make Natural Cleaners

Make Natural Cleaners

Keeping your home clean can actually be a pretty toxic experience if you use the typical chemical concoctions that are sold as cleaners these days.

Ingredients like ammonia and bleach are extremely harsh, and the fumes linger in your home long after you've done your cleaning. Many less pronounceable substances are mixed in for good measure (like maybe some dimethyl ethylbenzyl ammonium chloride or trisodium nitrilotriacetate), even though many have been linked to increased cancer rates. Not only do they affect the air quality in your home, these substances end up in the water supply. You can imagine what that will do to the environment.

All you really need around the house is vinegar, baking soda and salt. You can get vinegar at the grocery store in large jugs, and a bulk store should carry baking soda and salt in larger quantities. These three natural ingredients can create a variety of cleaning products that will keep your home clean without the noxious mess.

You may need to add a little elbow grease to get the same level of sparkling clean. Still, it's a small price to pay to green up your home.

Need some anti-bacterial action? Well, vinegar usually helps kill any bacteria because of the acid, but it's not very necessary. Our environment needs to have its usual compliment of microbes and we're not any healthier by sterilizing all our home surfaces.

Best of all, you will save a lot of money by making your own. The ingredients are all very cheap and can replace so many products. Just think of what you'll do with all that empty cabinet space once you've dumped a dozen bottles of commercial cleaners. And by "dumped" we mean that you have disposed of them properly at a waste disposal depot.

Fact

A good sink or tub cleaner can be made from:

1/4 cup of **baking soda** mixed with **1/2** cup of **vinegar**. Use a **rag** and **scrub** all your bathroom troubles away.

If you really **need more** scrubbing power, add a few pinches of **table salt**.

Try More Natural Insect Sprays

Try More Natural Insect Sprays

Do you still grab the usual bug sprays when you hit the outdoors? Be aware that their toxic chemicals can have significant consequences for your health and environment.

The most common ingredient in conventional insect repellent sprays is DEET, which is the easier way of saying N,N-Diethyl-meta-toluamide. If you're outdoors often during hot months, you may start to see some side-effects from exposure to the toxins. DEET concentrations found in most repellents are actually not that harmful, but if you are often outdoors in the summer you may start to see some side-effects.

Using really high concentrations of DEET is definitely not a good idea, though you can sometimes buy products that go up to 100 percent DEET. Stay away from them.

DEET also accumulates in the local water, like other chemicals we use too often. This is where the problem begins. Consider a lake where hundreds of DEET-coated swimmers go for a dip on a summer's day. The EPA has declared that DEET is toxic to many forms of aquatic life.

If you want an alternative, various essential oils can be used in place of DEET. The most common ones are lemongrass, eucalyptus and peppermint. To help deter mosquitoes in a small area, like your own yard, try growing some citronella or burning citronella-based candles.

If you prefer a less DIY approach, there are a few natural products on the market like Bite Blocker and Green Ban that are DEET-free repellents. They aren't as strong, so expect to apply them more often.

You can also avoid the need for repellents by wearing long sleeves and hats when you are out in buggy weather. Try to stay indoors during dusk and dawn when the pests are out in full force.

Fact

If **worn for long hours** in hot weather, DEET can have neurological effects and mild symptoms including forgetfulness, confusion overall fatigue.

Make Your Yard Bee-Friendly

Does this sound a little odd to you? Well, encouraging bees to hang around your yard may not sound reasonable, but the truth is that the declining bee population has recently become a hot-button environmental topic. No bees means no pollination, which will do some serious damage to the world (and our food supply).

Nobody is certain of what is causing the bees to die off, but the leading theory is the overuse of pesticides in commercial farming. Scientists are also looking at various other pathogens and diseases as potential causes. Regardless of the cause, bee populations are dropping drastically.

Plant Bee-Positive Flowers
The first and easiest thing you can do is to make sure your yard has a few bee-friendly types of flowers in it. The more food you can supply for our poor bee friends, the better off they're going to be. Think about adding some of the following to your garden:

- crabapple
- blueberry
- coneflower
- asters
- lavender
- clover
- bee balm
- catnip
- chives
- sunflowers
- primrose
- borage
- cosmos

These are all gorgeous plants and their heavy pollen supplies will make the bees happy too. A shallow dish of water with some stones in it will also make a nice water source.

Nix the Insecticides
Chemicals that kill the pests in your garden are not going to help bees, whether you are targeting them or not. Keep the toxins out of your garden to make it a healthier place to live (for bees and yourself). Use more natural options for bug control, or just accept that you have to share your garden with a few extra insect guests.

Fact

Regardless of the cause, the **bee populations** are dropping drastically. There are roughly **half the number** of commercial bee colonies in the U.S. compared to 60 years ago.

Stop Printing Everything

The paperless office is still an unrealized ideal these days, even with the boom of electronic and digital communications. Do you get an important email and then immediately print it out for safe-keeping? All this digital correspondence is actually producing more paper in the office!

Though it's almost all recyclable, all that printed paper still equals wasted resources.

Establish a spot on your computer to save important files and emails. Back that folder up regularly, and your emails will be just as protected as if they were printed. Bookmark important websites instead of printing them.

Reduce the Font

Shrink the font to the smallest readable size. It can mean the difference between printing 3 pages or only needing 2.

Use Both Sides

This is a bigger one, and it should cut your paper usage by half. If your printer doesn't have the option, you can run each piece back through the printer as you're printing so that your document is double-sided.

Use Recycled Paper

Try to buy computer paper that has a high percentage of recycled content in it to help reduce the demand for new paper. Recycled computer paper is as bright and crisp as "new" paper and similar in cost.

Turn Off the Printer

Even if you remember to turn the computer off each night, the printer can easily be forgotten and left on for days at a time. Don't leave it in sleep mode either, just turn it off.

Fact

The average office employee will use **10,000 sheets of** computer paper each year.

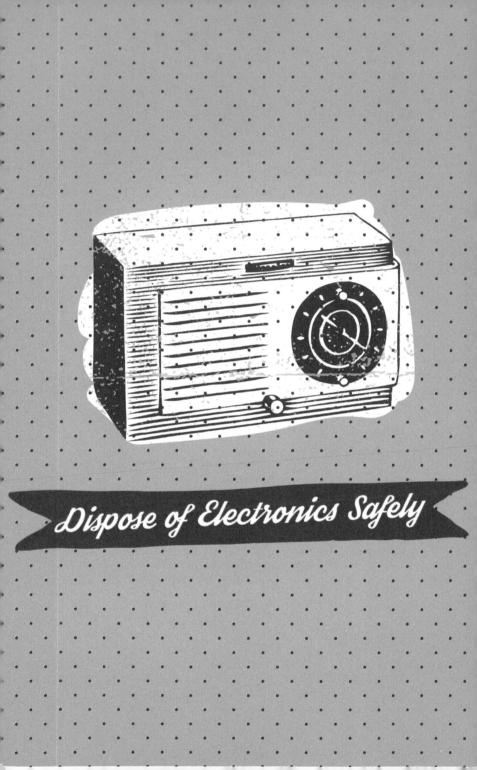

Dispose of Electronics Safely

Dispose of Electronics Safely

Our current world of computers and electronic devices has created a whole new realm of hazardous waste. Especially when people dump their gadgets as soon as a more recent model comes out.

If you want to be environmentally-conscious, hold on to your electronics until they are absolutely dead before moving on to the next gadget. But even then, what do you do with the old device? Your phone may be small, but its impact isn't trivial.

Your typical phone (or other computerized device) is going to contain toxins like lead, mercury, and cadmium as well as recoverable materials like copper, zinc, gold, and beryllium. The plastic casing is usually recyclable, too. The heavy metals are a hazard when they start to seep into the soil and water, and it's a huge waste to let those precious metals disappear into the garbage.

Check your local electronics store and ask if they have collecting depot for used items. They'll likely take a range of gadgets, not just phones. Most municipalities have a hazardous waste disposal depot as well, and that's a great place to drop off your old computers, phones or TVs.

If your device still has some life left, you can donate it so that it's used before being recycled for parts. For a million used phones, you can reclaim 35,000 pounds of copper, 772 pounds of silver and 75 pounds of gold. Secondwave Recycling is one option where you can send your phone to several worthy causes.

Before you recycle or donate any electronic devices, make sure to delete all your personal information. The batteries may need to be removed as well because they would be recycled separately.

Fact

The EPA estimates that **70%** of all the **toxic materials** that end up in landfills are electronic devices, and millions of them are **thrown away each year.**

Stop Using Disposable Razors

Stop Using Disposable Razors

They may last a little longer than a single shave, but plastic disposable razors are still a wasteful throw-away convenience.

As a mix of plastic and metal that is typically not recyclable, that means a whole lot of garbage. If this is an area you'd like to help out in, you have a few options.

Go Electric

An electric shaver is much better for the environment because there are no disposable components to go in the garbage. Yes it does use electricity, but the little shaver uses very little power and only runs for a few minutes a day. Compared to piles of discarded plastic, it's the greener option.

Some people feel that you don't get as close a shave. That may be true, though various models of shavers will give you different results.

Go Old-School

Old-fashioned safety razors are making a comeback. This doesn't mean one of those scary, long blades that cowboys used. A safety razor actually looks a lot like a disposable, and its design has a small bar in the head that protects the skin from the edge of the blade.

When dull, you just have to change the blade. It does still create a little trash, but the metal breaks down much easier than plastic and the volume of garbage is reduced. You can shave many times with a good metal blade before you have to change it.

You can do a bit of a compromise with this approach, and get the disposable variety where the handle is not thrown out and you just buy new cartridge heads for it. You'll reduce the amount of plastic you throw out, but not eliminate it entirely. Go the extra mile and buy a recyclable brand, too.

Fact

The **EPA** says that **2 billion** disposable razors are thrown out each year.

Shop Second-Hand

Shop Second-Hand

Everyone knows that shopping for second-hand or used items is a classic way to save money. You can get so many things that are in great shape at a fraction of the cost.

Did you ever think it's also an environmentally-friendly choice?

So many of our limited resources go into the making of stuff. Whether you're talking about clothes, furniture, toys, books, electronics, appliances or just nifty knick knacks, it all takes materials and energy to make. Resources are used up and pollution is created for absolutely every item you buy.

New products take a lot out of our planet, regardless of the industry.

And that's only half of the problem with new stuff. The other half of the trash equation is that people throw away their old items when they buy new ones. That produces more garbage for our poor landfills. By shopping second-hand, you're supporting a whole industry, and that will help keep these shops open for people to drop off their own used goods. It keeps the cycle going. And, of course, you should donate your used stuff to your local store instead of trashing it.

If you're getting visions of grubby garage sales, don't give up on the idea just yet. Many small thrift shops have a fun vintage air and funky feel. You're almost sure to find something one-of-a-kind. Larger second-hand stores are usually clean, well-lit and have a surprisingly wide inventory. Sometimes it's just like your typical department store.

So the next time you need something new, check out the local second-hand store first. It might take a few trips before you find what you're looking for, but the hunt is half the fun.

Fact

IKEA furniture store uses nearly **18 million cubic yards of lumber** every year to make its wares and a single pair of jeans uses up **2,900 gallons of water** during the dying processes.

Level ③

Green Thumb

Grow Your Own Food

Grow Your Own Food

No matter how black your thumb is or how small your home, there is always an opportunity to grow a little bit of food for yourself.

Every bit you can grow means a little less demand for our commercial agriculture industry. If you normally buy organic at a farmer's market, then you're already helping. If you are a conventional shopper, then growing your own will have great benefits. You can avoid treating your plants with pesticides or herbicides and protect our soil and water, and you're not adding pollution to the world with food transported to a store.

Herbs like oregano, lemon balm, thyme, chamomile and basil will all do fantastic on a sunny windowsill. It's a good first attempt at edible gardening. When you're ready to move on to something bigger, plan out a little vegetable garden.

One tomato plant can give you 30 or more pounds of fruit, and a single zucchini plant will probably bless you with more food than you can handle. You'll get more than a pound of beans with one little green bean plant. The point is, you can get a big harvest out of just a handful of potted plants on a patio or a garden.

If you're short on space, tall vining plants produce more than bush plants. With some support, a tall bean pole will give you more with less space. Same with tomatoes and peas. Maximize your harvest by thinking up!

Do a little research into what your plants need and get some seeds in the ground. There's no guarantee of a bumper crop, but odds are good that you'll have some home-grown goodies by the end of the season.

If you have kids, you can introduce them to the almost-forgotten art of growing your own food. The Earth can use a new generation that regains a little contact with the soil.

Fact

Most products **travel** more than **1,000 miles** before you find them on your **supermarket shelves**.

Revamp Your Lawn

Revamp Your Lawn

If you have a lovely green expanse of lawn outside of your home, you probably know how much work it is to maintain. But what about all that water you spend to maintain it?

While effective, it would be a little extreme to just pave over the lawn completely. For something less drastic, start thinking about water-friendly landscaping.

Create a few extra cobblestoned or gravelled paths, or perhaps a small wooden deck if you don't already have one. Gardens can be planted with flowers that handle dry weather better and require less watering.

If you want to create more flower beds, use a heavy layer of mulch to hold more moisture. You'll do less weeding too. Rock gardens, ponds, statuary and other decorative items can all take the place of some of your grass, and they add creativity to your garden.

Another option is to change the grass entirely. Many low-growing plants are better in dry weather than the usual lawn grass, so you could remove the sod in some parts of your yard and plant things like stonecrop or creeping rosemary.

Change your watering habits, too. If you're using a sprinkler, make sure the water is only reaching your plants, and don't let timers run indiscriminately. Also consider investing in a newer irrigation system. Some have sensors so that the sprinklers run only when the soil is dry.

Fact

According to the **EPA**, the average home uses more than **50 gallons** per day just to keep their lawns happy. As a nation, that's getting close to **9 billion gallons** every single day.

Eliminate Phantom Loads

Eliminate Phantom Loads

A phantom load is also known as standby power. Even when they're turned off, your devices are still using power. It's a very small amount of power, but each device adds up.

Older devices (pre-2010) could use up to 15W even while turned off, while modern electronics are now trying to reduce that to 1W or less. If you have TVs, computers, small appliances, stereo systems or any other large electric devices from before 2010, you are probably losing power every day and you don't even know it.

Not only are you paying for that power, it means more fossil fuels are being burned to generate it. Americans are losing billions of kWh in energy every year due to these hidden wastes.

Unplug your devices when they're not in use. For hard-to-reach plugs, use a power bar with its own on/off switch. Arrange the bar so you can still reach it behind the TV. When you turn off the TV, flip the switch on the power bar as well.

It may not be necessary to do this every time you use a device, but it could be an option to shut everything down at work and at night. Look at standby power usage next time you shop for an appliance or device too, so you aren't bringing more power vampires into the house.

Fact

An average home will be losing **2 to 4 kWh** each day in total to these power vampires. That's more than **1000 kWh** of electricity being wasted every year.

Get the Right Bulb

Get the Right Bulb

The push to switch from "old-fashioned" incandescent light bulbs is an old issue, but some folks are still resistant to changing. We've actually moved past CFL bulbs to the even newer LED lights. If you're confused about the various bulb options, now's the time to get to know your lights.

The old incandescent bulbs have a glass bulb and wire filament inside. Most people would consider them to be the standard light bulb. They don't last very long, use a lot of power, and produce a lot of heat. A 60W bulb will last about 1,200 hours and use 60 watts worth of power. Environmentally speaking, they are the worst bulbs you can choose.

CFL bulbs come in different shapes, but the most common is the little spiral tube kind that is about the same size as an incandescent. There are a couple of downsides to the now-common CFL. They may not operate in colder temperatures, which makes them lousy for outdoor use. They also contain a tiny bit of mercury, so dead bulbs need to be properly disposed of at a hazardous waste outlet. Still, they are a great environmental choice.

Now enter the newer LED bulbs. CFLs were a good improvement, but LEDs are proving to be even better. An LED light will use less power than incandescent bulbs and last for more than 50,000 hours. Unlike the CFLs, they're not toxic and won't be slowed down by cold weather. Still a little new to the household lighting world, these types of bulbs are getting easier to find.

Next time you need to shop for bulbs, keep these facts in mind before making your decision. The CFLs and LEDs will cost more up front, but the savings (in energy and cost) will add up very quickly.

 Fact

for the same amount of light as a **60W bulb,** → a **CFL bulb** will only use **14 Watts** and produce half as much heat.

It will also keep going for nearly **8,000** hours.

Don't Miss These Recyclables

Don't Miss These Recyclables

Unless you're some kind of blue box ninja, there is a good chance you're letting a few recyclables slip past you into the landfill. According to the EPA, about 75% of our garbage is recyclable but only 30% actually makes it to the bin.

Not all curbside programs accept the same materials, so check with your local collectors regarding these items:

Tetrapaks - Better known as "juice boxes."

Wire hangers - Only some collectors accept these since they can get tangled in the machine.

Aerosol cans - Some programs may recycle these if they're empty.

Aluminum foil - You can recycle plain sheets of foil, pie plates, or food trays as long as they are not heavily soiled with food.

For plastic items, check the numbers inside the little recycling symbols. Items labeled 3 or 7 are usually not acceptable.

Fact

| 1 | 2 | 3 | 4 | 5 | 6 | 7 |

1 (PET plastic)
Soft drink bottles, peanut butter jars, some kinds of microwave food trays

2 (HDPE plastic)
Milk and juice jugs, detergent bottles

3 (vinyl and PVC)
Shampoo bottles, many kinds of clamshell packages, deli wraps

4 (LDPE)
Some squeeze bottles, most kinds of plastic bags

5 (PP)
Margarine and yogurt tubs, many kinds of plastic bottles

6 (PS)
Meat trays, foam packing peanuts, CD cases

7 (other)
Plastic other than the first 6

Stop Using Disposables

Stop Using Disposables

Do you have products in your house that you use once and then just pitch in the trash? You probably have a few, and that's where you can make a little change to reduce how much garbage you're creating. Surely you've already given up plastic cutlery and paper plates, but here are a few more steps you can take at home.

The idea of carrying a refillable water bottle is rather trendy right now, and it is a much better choice than using single-serve plastic bottles. Don't comfort yourself by thinking that it's fine because you recycle all your bottles. A lot of oil is being used to create the plastic in the first place, and a lot of energy is still expended to recycle. Overall, Americans use more than 30 billion plastic water bottles each year. Just stop using them.

Paper towels can really add to your trash output, so stop using those too. The average person tosses out more than 700 pounds of paper products per year. Instead, keep a supply of rags or cloth towels in your kitchen. And don't be fooled by people who say you're wasting even more energy with the extra laundry. It's still the greener choice.

If you are really dedicated to getting rid of your household paper products, start carrying a handkerchief instead of reaching for a Kleenex. It might not the best option during a messy cold season, but it's worth a try.

Those disposable dusting cloths and one-use mopping pads are a fairly recent invention that is adding to our garbage woes. Just go back to the traditional dusting cloth and a handy sponge mop.

Resealable plastic storage bags (like Ziplock) shouldn't be tossed after one use. Wash them up when you do the dishes and you can zip them up for a dozen or more uses. Even lightly used pieces of aluminum foil can be wiped off and reused.

Fact

If everyone in the USA ditched **just one single roll of paper towel** from their lives, it would save more than **half a million trees.**

Try a Trashless Lunch

Try a Trashless Lunch

Kids and adults alike are packing lunches to save money and eat better. But if your bagged lunches include pre-wrapped and single-serve foods, you're adding to our environmental woes.

Though juice boxes are sometimes recyclable, carry your juice or water in a Thermos or reusable bottle. Skip the straw, too. They're unnecessary and create a lot of wasted plastic.

Plastic cutlery should be replaced by something non-disposable. Metal silverware is fine for adults, but may not be safe for children. If you do use plastic, try to clean and reuse it. Avoid paper napkins by using a cloth instead, they're just as effective.

If you're composting at home, any organic stuff should come home with you unless your school or workplace has its own compost bin.

To package your own food, buy little plastic containers or fabric snack bags. Instead of using pre-packaged cookies or snack cakes, buy a larger box and toss a few cookies into your own container. Chunks of cheese, carrot sticks, pieces of fruit, crackers and more can be packed up yourself to reduce plastic packaging.

Think before grabbing a straw, most drinks don't need it. Try a reusable instead. You can purchase glass or metal straws and avoid adding to the plastic problem.

What are you packing your lunches in? A reusable bag or box will last for years (well, at least one year for rough kids), and they are more durable than a flimsy paper bag.

Like most of these green tips, you'll save money. It's far cheaper to buy large quantities of food that you divide yourself than buying single-serve packs.

A few plastic pieces may not seem like a lot of trash, but since lunches are part of daily life, it adds up. Once you have the containers and bags handy at home, packing a lunch will still be a snap.

Fact

A typical lunch creates about **1/3** of pound **of trash**.

By the end of the year, that will add nearly

100 lbs **of** garbage to the landfill.

Switch to E-flyers

Switch to E-flyers

Most of us hate the junk mail that clogs up our mailboxes, except for the great deals. We hate missing a good bargain as much as the waste. It's a tricky catch-22 problem for the environmental enthusiast.

With most major retailers offering digital flyers, it's easy to switch to an e-flyer. Go to the company's website and sign up to get them via email. Most are digital versions of the actual paper flyer (complete with page turning), so you'll get the same information.

You still need to get rid of the paper flyers, so put a sign on your mailbox asking that no flyers be delivered. Most route carriers will honor your request.

Not only are you saving huge wads of paper (and all that high-gloss ink), as companies start to use eflyers more often, there will be fewer drivers out there delivering all that paper. That means less fuel waste and vehicle emissions. Definitely an all-around win.

The paper savings are pretty obvious with this tip, and you'll avoid getting mail you don't want. Recycling is definitely a good choice, but stopping the flyers for good is best.

Look for Organic Cotton

Look for Organic Cotton

We tend to think "organic" when it comes to our food. Maybe it should be something we need to look for in our clothing, too.

Cotton may seem wholesome and natural as a raw material, but it's carrying a pretty big secret. It's a very environmentally unfriendly crop to grow. It is very susceptible to insect pests so there is a heavy use of pesticides on every acre of conventionally-grown cotton. It's considered to be the "dirtiest" crop there is, in terms of how many toxins are sprayed on it.

That's having quite an effect on the environment, but what about right in your own home? Clothing is usually pretty free of any residues, especially if you give your new things a wash when you get them home. On the other hand, a lot of cotton bedding will have some residues left behind.

Then there's the GMO problem. Genetically-modified cotton crops are now taking up 20% of the world's cotton production, which may have a terrible impact on the environment as they interact with native species. Lastly, cotton needs a huge amount of water to grow and for processing. About 2 pounds of cotton will need up to 20,000 quarts of water.

Even organic cotton will use a lot of water. But along with growing cotton without all the chemicals, many organic farmers are moving towards cotton crops that rely on rain-fed water systems instead of pumped irrigation.

Try to buy some of your clothing with organic cotton to help support the cleaner cotton farms. You'll be saving badly needed water resources.

Fact

In fact, the World Wildlife Fund says that even though cotton only represents **2.4%** of the world's crop land, it needs up to **24%** of the planet's agricultural pesticides.

Don't Idle & Don't Drive Alone

Don't Idle & Don't Drive Alone

Don't idle! In other words, don't just sit there with your car running for no good reason.

Now, that doesn't mean you should shut down the engine at every stop sign.

Even when parked, a running car is still spewing the same air pollutants as it does when driving down the road. Carbon monoxide, nitrogen oxide and other volatile organic fumes are wafting into the atmosphere, and you're not even getting any travel out of it.

It may not seem like much at first, but all those idle minutes and miles add up. The Environmental Defense Fund estimates that you are wasting about 1/5 of a gallon per hour of idling. Considering the cost of gas these days, that's just wasted money. And don't be fooled: modern cars don't need to be warmed up in cold weather. Starting and stopping your engine won't damage it, either.

Better yet, avoid driving at all. Public transit can help out if you live and work right in the same large city, otherwise, you're stuck in your car. Join forces with friends or neighbors (or even strangers if you want), and share the commute.

You'll reduce pollution and congestion on the roads by using only one car. Designated carpool lanes may even get you to work more quickly. If you don't want to pick everyone up at home, set up a place to meet.

By rotating who does the driving, it means everyone else gets a break from the added stress of navigating traffic. Couldn't we all use a little less stress on a workday?

Not only are you doing Mother Earth a favor, you can have a little casual social time with colleagues on the way to work. And if you're not the chatty type, you can catch up on Twitter.

Fact

Depending on the vehicle, a single driver will use **400 gallons** of gas each year and create **8,000 pounds** of carbon dioxide.

Level 4

Eco Expert

Get Biking

If you have great public transportation options, this might not apply. But if you spend a lot of time in your car for short errands, why not get a new set of wheels?

The benefits of biking are too many to list. It's not only good for the environment, it's fantastic for your body.

A standard car spits out fumes that contain carbon dioxide, fine particles of metal and oil, and a mix of nitrogen and sulfur compounds. These hazardous fluids can harm the soil and the air. For the usual driver, that can equal more than 6 tons of carbon every year. On top of their pollution, cars need gasoline and oil, non-renewable resources, just to run.

Your bicycle is fueled by your own body energy and releases no pollution. It might take longer to get to your destination and you can't carry much, but it's a great option for most trips. Even if you still use your car to get groceries, every errand you can replace with a bike will help our air.

An initial investment of getting a good bike and accessories will be your only cost. Repairs may come up, but they'll be cheaper than maintaining a car.

If you are somewhat new to bike riding, don't try to tackle a commute along a busy highway. An actual bike path will help you ease into a regular routine of getting around by bike. Add a basket or even a small wagon and you can even carry some purchases during your trip.

Until your body gets used to being your vehicle's engine, it might be a bit tiring to bike around all day. Just think about how much good you're doing the world, and you'll soon enjoy the ride.

Fact

Every gallon of gas your car burns will create nearly **20 lbs of carbon** put out into the atmosphere.

Try Dimmer Switches

Try Dimmer Switches

Modern light bulbs like CFLs and LEDs don't use a lot of power compared to the old-fashioned incandescent bulbs, but there are always more ways you can reduce your energy consumption.

The idea is simple. Dimming a light bulb will reduce the amount of power it uses without having to permanently change the bulb to a lower wattage. A family room light fixture might be a good candidate for a dimmer. If you're just sitting around watching TV, a dimmed light is all you need. You can still get full brightness when you're playing cards or a board game.

You may have heard that these don't really help that much. While this was actually true a few decades ago, modern dimmers do cut down power usage, so don't let someone's out-of-date facts discourage you.

Before you hit the home improvement store for switch hardware, take a look at your light bulbs. Most people have CFL bulbs in their homes, which may be a problem if they are not compatible with the dimmer. Older CFLs cannot be used with dimmers at all. Newer ones will work as long as the dimmer switch is intended for use with CFLs. LED bulbs can also be used with the appropriate dimmers.

It doesn't take an engineering degree to change out a switch, and you can probably do it on your own with a few basic tools. A video tutorial might be helpful too. Even if you have to pay someone, you will end up saving money in the long run.

How much electricity you can save will really depend on how much dimming you do with each bulb. If you have a 15W bulb dimmed to around half power, it will only use 7W or so. Every saved watt makes a difference.

Fact

The average USA household uses around **7,500** kWh per year.

Use Rechargeable Batteries

Use Rechargeable Batteries

Most electronic devices today are rechargeable, but there are still plenty of "old school" products in your home that rely on battery power. Toys, flashlights, remote controls, clocks and various other household gadgets still use the standard AA or AAA batteries for power. And after a while, those used batteries can really pile up.

Batteries are loaded with acids and heavy metals like mercury, lead and cadmium. They are some of the most harmful things to put in a landfill. But rather than dumping all of your battery-powered devices, switch to rechargeable batteries. Each rechargeable battery can replace up to 1,000 conventional batteries before it wears out and won't hold a charge anymore. They will also save a lot of hazardous material from the landfill.

You can get all the usual battery sizes in rechargeable format. The most common are AAA and AA, but even C, D and even 9-volt are available. Some chargers can handle any size and some will only work with one kind of battery. Take a look around your house and see what you use the most. The average house has 20 to 40 different battery powered devices in it, so there may be more than you think.

You'll need a collection of batteries and a good charger to cover all your devices. Keep extras so that you have some that are fully charged to use while the dead ones are plugged in. Most rechargeables are NiMH these days (nickel-metal hydride) and they are the best format to get. Avoid older NiCd (nickel-cadmium) batteries as the cadmium can damage the environment.

There are up-front costs, but you'll see monetary savings add up when you realize you're not buying more batteries every couple of months. And you'll keep hundreds of toxic materials out of the environment.

Fact

Three billion single-use household **batteries** end up in the **garbage** every year in the USA, and they are loaded with **acids** and **heavy metals** like mercury, lead and cadmium.

Refill Your Toner

Your printer can be an environmentally un-friendly part of your home or office, but a few tips can help green it right up. Those plastic toner cartridges contain toxic chemicals and reusable materials. That's a lot of wasted resources going to the trash.

The main problem with refilling your own toner is that the companies that make toner cartridges want you to buy more of them. So that generally means that these things aren't made to be refilled. A little ingenuity can easily help you go green. And you're not alone—companies that sell the toner powder can usually walk you through the process.

First, you have to get the right toner. There is no generic stuff, it all has to match your model of printer or you risk gumming the whole thing up and ruining the entire machine. The heat created by the machine has to match the composition of the toner or it won't fuse properly to the paper.

You will need to drill or burn a small hole in the right side of your cartridge. Fill up the reservoir inside with the toner powder, then seal the hole. If done right, your newly filled cartridge will work as well as a new one and last about as long. Just be careful when you do the filling. The powder is very fine and can be a supreme mess if spilled.

If you don't want to alter your cartridges, you can see if the manufacturer has a take-back program. Many will accept their cartridges back using prepaid shipping labels (with no cost to you) to be reused by the company. Every 100,000 cartridges recycled means 40 tons of plastic and 10 tons of aluminium are kept out of the garbage.

 Fact

Approximately **375** million **cartridges** are trashed each year in the USA, and that is a lot of plastic, metal and toxic chemicals being **wasted.**

Ladies, Try Cloth Pads

This can be a bit of a delicate subject, but it's worth a mention because this is a change that will have a big impact on your trash production. Cloth diapers are fairly mainstream, so why not cloth pads for your period?

Besides the garbage produced, the bleaching process makes the manufacturing of pads fairly toxic too. Why contribute to that?

There are a few reusable options for your monthly needs, and cloth pads are one of the easiest to use. They are shaped like a standard pad, usually with snaps and wings. Some may have a waterproof liner and some may not. You wear them like a disposable pad and then toss them in the laundry.

Like with cloth diapers, a few tips can help out here to make the transition work easier. For one thing, it is a very good idea to let your used pads soak in clear water if you're not doing laundry right away. But other than that, they shouldn't need special care. Many women who have switched say they are much more comfortable to wear, too.

There are several great brands (GladRags, Wemoon and Lunapads) and they come in a variety of sizes, just like the disposable kinds. You can get creative with fun fabrics or stick with the unbleached cotton types, and a supply of about a dozen should suffice. They may seem expensive at first (anywhere from $4 to $20 per pad), but you'll see savings after a few months of not buying the disposable ones.

Will you use more water and electricity with this extra laundry? Yes, but you'll still be doing the Earth (and yourself) a favor.

Fact

On average, a typical woman will use and throw away **15,000 pads (or tampons)** during her lifetime. That can equal nearly **300 pounds of** waste ending up at the dump.

Try Using Cloth Diapers

Try Using Cloth Diapers

Disposable diapers are one of the most convenient products you can buy. Nothing makes a parent's life easier than just tossing a dirty diaper in the garbage. Ever think about where all those diapers end up?

Since they are completely non-recyclable, every single diaper will go to your local landfill. That's a lot of bulky garbage, and the production of diapers also uses a ton of resources and water. They are a very non-green product.

Cloth diapers are gaining popularity for their Earth-friendly nature and the huge cost savings. Don't confuse them with the old-fashioned types your grandmother used. Today, a typical cloth diaper is made with snaps or velcro, has fitted elastic legs, and will come on and off just as easily as a disposable. You won't need to fiddle around with diaper pins.

Don't let the "yuck" factor sway you. Once you get into a routine with cloth diapers, you'll find you hardly handle them at all. Keep a diaper pail near your change area (with a tight lid!) and dump the whole thing in the washing machine. Air dry the diapers for some extra environmental savings. The added water use is still a far greener choice that using conventional diapers.

Concerned about the "solid waste" (aka poop) in dirty diapers? Soft paper liners can be added to each diaper and lifted out along with the solid mess to be disposed of separately. Though the liners are disposable, you are still creating a tiny fraction of the trash. If they are just wet at change time, the liners are usually washable too.

For the lucky parents who have babies in their lives, cloth diapers will help the environment and your budget. There is an upfront cost, but you can save more than $1,000 by the time you're potty training by going with cloth. And if you can hand-me-down the diapers for another child, the savings will add up.

Expect to toss at least **8,000 diapers** before your little one is finally potty-trained.

Limit to NO Antibiotics

Limit to NO Antibiotics

The discovery of antibiotics has changed the face of medicine, and help us conquer a whole host of diseases. But those days, antibiotics are creating their own problems.

People are taking antibiotic medications for way too many things, and it's starting to impact the evolution of the microscopic world. The diseases are developing resistance to the drugs and that is going to make treatment more difficult in the future.

Antibiotics are getting into the groundwater from our garbage cans and even our urine. This a two-fold problem. It's aiding the development of "super-bugs," while traces of antibiotics are killing off the normal bacteria that we need in the environment.

To help limit the amount of these chemicals in our water supply, try not to take antibiotics unless it's truly necessary. Don't ask the doctor for antibiotics just because you have a cold. It isn't going to help much anyway. Dispose of any leftover antibiotics at the pharmacy. Don't toss or flush them.

It's not only humans adding antibiotics to the environment. Many commercially farmed livestock also take loads of antibiotics, which is compounding the problem even more. To decrease demand, try to eat organic meat as much as possible or meat that is labelled antibiotic-free.

Fact

Not long ago, the U.S Geological Survey measured the **water quality** in the natural streams across **30 states**. They found traces of pharmaceutical medications in **80%** of their samples.

Avoid GMOs

Avoid GMOs

This environmental problem didn't even exist a few years ago. Today, you can barely read a newspaper without finding a story on GMOs and, unfortunately, they're bad news.

First, what the heck is a GMO? The term GMO stands for "genetically modified organism," and has been created artificially through gene splicing. It involves the mixing of genes from more than one species to create a "superior" plant or animal.

The most common purpose of a GMO is to create a plant that is very resistant to herbicides, so that farmers can douse their fields with toxins and not harm their crops.

Do not confuse this with the natural process of cross-breeding that people have been using for centuries. GMOs represent a very unnatural creation that comes from a laboratory.

We have no idea how GMOs are going to interact with the environment. Are they going to cross-breed with wild or native species and further spread fish or bacteria genes in our food chain? What are these mutated crops going to do to our bodies? The industry insists they're safe, but do you trust their judgement? If it turns out these foods are harmful to us, we are going to be in serious trouble.

You'll find GMOs in crops like corn, alfalfa, canola, cotton, and soy. This isn't some future prediction, a majority of these foods are already GMOs in the United States. More than 60 countries have banned these products, but the USA doesn't even require labelling. Basically, that means you have no idea what you're eating.

Find products that are certified with non-GMO ingredients or stick with organic foods. Part of the organic certification is that there can be no GMO ingredients.

Add your voice to this hot-button issue. Sign petitions, contact government officials, and join in protests against the spread of GMOs. If you're not an activist at heart, simply avoid buying these foods. Reducing demand is still an effective tool against the industry.

Fact

For example, nearly **90% of all the corn** grown in the US is a GMO of some kind.

Wrap Gifts the Green Way

Wrap Gifts the Green Way

Not to be a Grinch, but the holidays are notorious for creating mountains of wasted paper garbage. Most wrapping paper is high-gloss so it's completely unrecyclable and gets dumped in the landfill.

If you want to make your holidays a little more environmentally friendly, you can try some of these tips.

1 If you already have paper, reuse it. Be delicate when you unwrap gifts so each piece can be used to wrap other gifts in the future. Gift bags tend to work better for reusing than paper wrap. When you have a decent collection, you can keep reusing bags for years.

2 Use paper that is made from recycled material and can be recycled. With a little creativity, you can even wrap gifts in newspaper. It won't be quite as colorful, but it'll do the trick.

3 You can also use reusable cloth wraps for your gifts and bypass all the paper completely. Cloth bags will work really well and last a long time. A large square of fabric can be used to wrap a gift just like paper and either safety pins or creative knotting can hold its shape. A little Internet search for "furoshiki" (the Japanese art of cloth wrapping) will give you plenty of ideas. You can buy pre-cut fabric sheets or make your own. Get extra environmental points by cutting fabric from old sheets or clothes.

4 You can also green up your holidays by simply giving fewer gifts. Do we really need more stuff? Gift cards and cash don't need much wrapping. Instead of giving 8 small gifts, plan on giving just one larger one.

Store your salvaged paper, bags or cloth wraps until next year along with your holiday decorations and it will become second-nature to use them. It will also save you money when you don't have to shop for yet another armload of wrapping paper.

 Fact

Over the Christmas season, Americans throw out more than **25 million** tons of additional garbage, much of which is gift wrapping related packaging.

Get Hip about Hemp

Get Hip about Hemp

Hemp isn't just for hippies anymore. As a fast growing plant that creates a renewable resource for paper, fuel, food and a wide range of other products, you have to wonder why it's not a major crop across the country. The fact that it's a variant of Cannabis is the problem.

Some countries grow hemp commercially (like China, France, and Canada), so there is already a growing industry for its use. But in the United States, it's only legal to import it, not grow it.

If you can look past the drug connection, hemp is a better resource than most of the crops or materials we are using now. The list of possibilities is endless. Let's just examine hemp in two areas: paper and fuel.

Paper is usually made with wood pulp from trees. Though trees are a renewable resource, it can take years for a crop of trees to reach the size needed for the pulping industry.

The pulp of hemp is much lighter than wood pulp, so you can make paper without the chlorine bleaching process. It's more durable and can be recycled twice as often as conventional paper. Hemp also requires virtually no herbicides or pesticides, and it needs very little water. Cotton, on the other hand, uses about 50 times as much water to produce the same amount of fiber (yes, hemp fiber can be used in clothing too).

What about fuel? This is still a developing area for hemp, but its seeds have a high volume of oil that can be processed into a biofuel similar to ethanol. Fermentation of the stalks can also make a form of fuel oil. Unlike corn, it's an Earth-friendly crop that won't destroy the land.

Unfortunately, the stigma attached to marijuana usage has ruined its reputation. So what can you do? Buy hemp products and contact your representatives about making it a legal crop in the United States.

Buy Shade Grown Coffee

Buy Shade Grown Coffee

Even hard-core green enthusiasts may find this one to be an unusual tip. Most coffee grown today by the larger producers is grown in fields that have been completely razed of trees to maximize the amount of sunlight the plants receive. Unfortunately, this practice is starting to have serious effects on the landscape. As the constant growth of coffee has depleted the soil, the lack of shade trees has caused a major decline in local bird populations. These areas are all places that were once very heavily forested, and tree removal has completely destroyed the ecosystems.

The ironic fact is that coffee grown with a canopy of trees still in place actually requires less chemical fertilizers and pesticides as well. The bird populations take care of most of the bugs without any effort on the farmer's part. It's a much better arrangement for everyone.

Coffee does grow just fine under shade, but it makes field maintenance a little tougher for the big mechanized farmers. Shade-grown coffee is only slightly more expensive than the conventional brands, though it depends on what type of coffee you are used to drinking.

You might also find coffee grown this way labelled as "bird-friendly" coffee as well. It's basically the same thing either way. While you're at it, see if it's a fair-trade product. It means that the farmers were paid a fair and appropriate wage for their work, and though it may not help the environment, it's still a good thing to do.

Fact

Over the past **10 years**, the bird populations in coffee-growing regions have dropped by **20%**.

Pick Greener House Paint

Pick Greener House Paint

We're not talking about the color, but the content. Conventional paint is chock full of toxic chemicals, which you can usually smell after you've freshly painted a room. Next time you want to redecorate, make a more environmental choice.

All those nasty fumes you get when you paint are from the volatile organic compounds (or VOCs) that make up standard interior paints. They are included in paint formulas to make it dry faster and prevent mold. Not only are VOCs unnecessary, they're terrible for the environment.

When you start to breathe them, you will get headaches, eye and throat irritation, dizziness and nausea. There are actually dozens of different compounds that fall under the title of "VOC" and some are even known to be likely carcinogens.

These chemicals are actually present in household cleaners and adhesives as well. The average home has higher than normal levels of these chemicals, and they are even higher after a new coat of paint.

Even if you keep yourself away from the fumes, they're still seeping into the outside air. It doesn't address the actual problem.

Instead, eliminate them altogether. Choose brands of paint that have no VOCs or low levels of them in order to cut down on air pollution. Old-fashioned milk paint is making a comeback with the eco-minded. True milk paints are sold as a powder that you mix yourself, and they do in fact contain milk proteins (which work as natural binders).

Minimize how much paint you use and decide how many coats you really need. Once you're done painting, dispose of leftovers at a hazardous waste depot. If your cans are empty, they may be recyclable as well.

Fact

These **chemicals** are actually present in a lot of other things besides paint, like **household cleaners** and **adhesives** for example. Overall, the average house has a level of these fumes that is **2 to 5 times** higher than the outside air.

Get Some Green Power

While it would be nice to get off the grid and have handy solar panels on your roof to power your home, it's not that feasible for your average person. Prices for solar panels are coming down, but a full system is still out of most people's budgets. Can you help the Earth with some clean power? Yes, you sure can.

Some utility companies now get their power from clean renewable sources, so you can just switch providers to one of these greener companies and be happy that you're not contributing to climate change every time you turn on the light.

It's one of the simplest things you can do, but it has a big impact because your entire household's worth of electrical power is off the grid and nothing in your day-to-day life has to change.

Still, finding a new electrical provider isn't as easy as switching brands of breakfast cereal. In some parts of the country, you might be completely out of luck while other areas might have several choices open to you.

In the southeastern states, you can check out Duke Energy. All of their power comes from renewable sources. Some mainstream utility companies offer renewable power plans along with their usual fossil fuel plans. Portland General Electric, for example, has more than one green energy plan you can switch to.

You do need to read up on the details. Most mainstream companies aren't literally providing clean power, they are just trying to "offset" your carbon usage. Shop around!

Fact

The average household in the U.S. uses about **11,000 kWh of electricity** each year (it can vary a lot by state and climate). If you translate that into carbon emissions, you're adding nearly **5,000 pounds of carbon** to the atmosphere annually just using electricity.

Start Composting

Start Composting

It's almost trendy these days to have a compost bin of some size in your yard, but not everyone has gotten on board. For many, throwing out food scraps seems trivial.

The truth is adding your kitchen garbage isn't as harmless as it seems. While it's all organic matter, the airless environment of a landfill doesn't allow it to break down quickly. The result is that landfills are producing huge quantities of methane, which is a known greenhouse gas (and a far worse one than carbon dioxide). Landfills contribute about 20 percent of the entire country's production of methane, which is why there is an ongoing movement to get people to start composting.

You don't need a huge yard, and you won't have a big smelly pile of rotting garbage to deal with either. It's easy and harmless. A commercial bin is an easy purchase, or you can drill some holes in an old garbage can for a DIY option. Add your kitchen waste (no meat or dairy), along with grass clippings, pulled weeds and even small quantities of shredded paper.

Keep it damp in hot, dry weather and you should have a nicely active compost unit in no time. Give it a stir when it start to fill up, so that there is air through the mixture. Adding in paper and plants will keep it from getting smelly.

By composting, you'll create rich, natural fertilizer for your plants. If you don't have a garden, find a friend with one. If you'd prefer to leave composting to others, many cities now accept scraps for larger composting projects. See what's available in your area.

You can also do your best to throw out as little food as possible in the first place and reduce the amount of organic waste coming out of your home.

Fact

Landfills contribute about **20 percent** of the entire country's production of methane, which is why there is an ongoing movement to get people to start composting.

Harvest Some Rainwater

Harvest Some Rainwater

Our clean water supplies are dwindling. More and more parts of the country suffer from droughts as temperatures slowly creep upward every summer. If you want to reduce how much water your home draws from city supplies, try gathering up some rainwater.

Water for laundry, drinking and toilet use is harder to supplement with rainwater. But you can carve a big chunk out of your water usage if you use harvested water in the garden and lawn. If you are really handy with plumbing, you could even divert some to your washing machine.

All you need is a large barrel placed under a downspout. If you want to get fancy, you can get a barrel with a lid and a spigot to attach a hose. A spigot will help you access the water a little easier. Dunking a watering can into the barrel will also fill it up nicely.

If you can find an empty barrel from a food or drink manufacturer, they work well and cost less than a water barrel from a store. Make sure that your second-hand barrel never held anything toxic. A garbage can may be tempting, but they're not thick enough to stand the pressure of the water.

The usual type of barrel will hold around 55 gallons of water. If you were to have one at every corner of your house, that would give you about 200 gallons of free water once they are filled.

Though you don't need a lid, it can be helpful to cut a piece of window screening to cover the top. Otherwise, you might have a bit of a problem with mosquitoes breeding in your water supply.

And not only is all this rainwater free, it's not chlorinated or fluoridated like municipal city water supplies. That's even better for your garden than tap water.

 Fact

The average person uses around **90 gallons** of water every day.

Raise a Few Chickens

Raise a Few Chickens

This might seem like a bit too "extreme" of a tip for anyone who isn't already living a rural lifestyle. Believe it or not, this is the latest trend in urban living.

There are actually several different benefits from having your own chickens. You will get a regular supply of all-natural eggs with no antibiotics or growth hormones involved, as well as a place to dispose of your kitchen scraps. They will also do wonders for the bug population in your yard.

Commercial egg farms are very harmful to the environment, and definitely unpleasant for the chickens. The main problem to the environment is the large concentration of waste and manure run-off that starts to pollute the local water systems.

More detailed information on raising backyard chickens is easy to find online, but here is a quick run-down of the basics:

 You will need a secure place for your chickens to live inside a little coop. A fenced-in area (or the whole yard, if you want) lets them get fresh air and eat plenty of grass and bugs. You can feed them scraps from the kitchen, but a bag of proper chicken food is important to keep them healthy. Without balanced nutrients, egg production will suffer.

 A good hen will give you 1 egg every other day. A great hen will lay one daily. So take that into account when you design your flock, though you probably won't have any shortage of neighbors who would appreciate surplus eggs.

Having a handful of chickens in your yard means you can enjoy your eggs guilt-free, and know that you aren't contributing to commercial chicken farms.

Install a Wood Stove

Install a Wood Stove

This is another of those tips that may not suit everyone, especially if you're on a tight budget. But if you're in the market for a new stove, keep it in mind.

Though the length of time it takes for a tree to reach harvestable size is many years, ultimately wood is a renewable resource whereas oil and natural gas is not. Even if you heat with electricity, there is a good chance that your power is coming from a coal or nuclear powered plant. Either way, you're using up precious fuel with each chilly month you are running the furnace.

Your stove's fossil fuel use depends on which variety you are using (oil, natural gas, propane) and the severity of your winter season. A home might burn several hundred thousands of cubic feet of gas each year. That is a lot of non-renewable fuel disappearing.

With a wood stove, you might use between two or three cords of wood. With just a few piles, you can save more than a thousand gallons of oil every year.

You should find a central point in your home (like a living room) and get a professional to help you with the specifics about installation. There need to be fire-proof surfaces under and surrounding the stove, and a proper chimney will need to be added. Once in place, you'll need to learn the fine art of managing a fire. Don't get discouraged if it gives you trouble at first. It can take a little experience.

If you are thinking about cutting costs a little and burning scrap wood, you can go ahead and do it as long as it's not painted. You also should avoid particle board or MDF. They have a whole host of chemicals in them that you don't want to start burning. But if you have a supply of "plain" scrap wood, go ahead.

Fact

A home in the northern United States might go through **1,000 gallons** of heating oil each winter.

The Dual-Flush Toilet

The Dual-Flush Toilet

This is a fairly simple tip that can save you a lot of water, but it may be expensive. Buying a new toilet probably isn't on your immediate to-do list unless you need one. But if you do, consider getting a dual-flush model.

Invented in 1980, these clever toilets let you control your water usage with each flush. This means less wasted water. A dual-flush toilet has the option to make a "mini flush" when you need less water, usually less than one gallon. A conventional toilet uses around 1 1/2 gallons of water every time you flush, not matter how much water you really need.

The premise is that you can still use the regular full flush when you have "solid waste" to dispose of, but then drop that down to a mini-flush when you don't. The best thing is that you really don't have to much of a change in your day-to-day life.

Most models have a double button on the top of the tank where you can pick your flushing preference, and some have an adjustable lever. Either way, they are simple to use.

These kinds of toilets are the norm in Australia (where they were invented) and are only just now gaining some traction in North America. They can cost a little more than a regular toilet, but prices are going down. In some cases, the dual-flush will cost the same.

If you do decide to switch out your toilet, make sure to dispose of your old one properly. See if there is a building supply store in your area that may take it or turn it into a unique garden planter.

Fact

Over the course of a year, a family can save **thousands of gallons** of water by using the smaller **flush cycle.**

Quit Smoking

Smoking has a far greater reach than your pocketbook or your health—it's a global environmental issue. There are so many ecological problems with cigarettes, it's hard to know where to start.

First, they use up a lot of resources. An entire tree is wasted to create 300 cigarettes. That includes the paper production as well as deforestation for tobacco crops. If you look at the carbon dioxide alone, smokers add about 3 billion tons to the atmosphere each year.

Next comes all the garbage that is created by smoking. Granted, most of a cigarette literally goes up in smoke, but the stubs and butts are left behind, too. People who just pitch their butts contribute to a large amount of litter. It's estimated that 1.7 billion pounds of cigarette butts are trashed each year.

Then there's the air pollution created every time you light up. A cigarette will give off hundreds of different chemicals when burned, many of which are known to be toxic to the environment. It's not just burning paper and tobacco! Tar fumes along with carbon monoxide, heavy metals and hydrogen cyanide are just a few. Pesticide residues are common on tobacco leaves, and those chemicals end up in the smoke as well.

Considering that smoking doesn't even serve any useful purpose, the choice should be obvious. There are many great tools out there to help you the addiction. You'll be helping yourself as well as the planet.

Fact

On a grander scale, the **5.6 trillion cigarettes** produced each year means that nearly **20 billion trees** have to be cut down.

Go Vegetarian

Go Vegetarian

The controversy about being an herbivore versus a carnivore is long and emotional. Right now, we'll set aside the moral reasons for giving up meat and look at how our eating habits impact the Earth. Any other judgements after that are up to you.

When it comes to the environmental impact of a meat-based diet, there are two main areas where livestock harm the planet: water consumption and land usage.

Producing wheat requires only a fraction of the gallons of water that go into meat production. With fresh water being in short supply through much of the world, this can equal a huge amount of unnecessary waste. The average American eats around 250 lbs of meat every year, so simply cutting down your steak intake will have a big impact.

What about land usage? Not only do herds of livestock take up large parcels of land, but the fields of feed crops (like corn or soy) are also part of the equation. Forests are removed to clear land for these purposes. In the USA alone, more than 250 million acres of forest have been cut down to make way for livestock-related agricultural land. The loss of trees harms the atmosphere and leaves soil open to more erosion.

If you want an eco-friendly diet but aren't keen on ditching all your meat, just make a few small changes. Try a meat-less entry one or two nights a week rather than give it all up. You can also focus on less resource-intensive meats like chicken or pork. Beef is typically the worst for eco-impact. Finding a local small-scale source for your meat is another option.

Fact

It can take over 2,000 gallons of **water** to produce a single pound of **beef**, but only **25** gallons to produce a pound of **wheat.**

Learn to Upcycle & Freecycle

They're the new buzzwords in green circles and they're more fun than recycling. "Upcycling" is a creative way to reuse things around the house so that you are throwing away less garbage. "Freecycling" is exactly what it sounds like: giving and getting things for free.

With upcycling, the idea is that you use your unwanted things to make something new and just as useful as the originals. Upcycling can be a great option for items that can't be recycled. A couple of old shirts, for instance, can make a quilt.

Being crafty is a better way to view all the "junk" we have at home. Sure, tossing empty plastic bottles into the blue bin is a good idea, but try to see them as raw materials for a useful creation. Even a simple jar can make a nifty pencil holder or vase. If you're not crafty, plenty of websites offer instructions and ideas to spur your creativity.

Freecycling is an appealing option for the frugal shopper. Online, people are giving away items they no longer want on sites like Freecycle.org. Furniture and kitchen appliances are the most common things you'll find, but clothing, toys, electronics, craft supplies, building materials and just about anything else might be given away.

The selection changes daily, so keep an eye out online. Most sites have pages for your city or area. When you see something you can use, just send a message to the owner and arrange for a pickup.

You can also post when you need something. With a simple post, you can possibly jog someone's memory about an item they had forgotten.

Freecycling creates a personal network between people who enjoy dealing in second hand things. You never know who you might meet.

By getting second-hand items or creating your own, you're saving resources by not creating a demand for more new stuff.

Research – Don't Fall for Hype

RESEARCH – Don't Fall for Hype

This tip is less concrete, and more of a shift in thinking. As you read the news about the latest product fads, don't let yourself get carried away by the latest "super foods." Do research before jumping on the bandwagon.

When a new super food ingredient hits the market, people go crazy over it because the health benefits seem endless. But no one mentions that thousands of acres of rainforest are being bulldozed to make room to grow it, or that whole villages are working in poverty to process it. A new kind of plastic may mean a reduced use of fossil fuels, but it may also create more pollution.

To use a more literal example: the wonder-grain quinoa. It's been the new hot food for a couple of years now, but what's the backstory? Well, only one small region in the Andes grows this crop, and the explosion in demand has ruined the local economy and is starting to harm the environment at the same time. Not to bash quinoa, but that's a major drawback to its benefits.

Another similar idea is coined in the word "greenwashing." This is when companies and manufacturers try to put a more environmentally-friendly face on their product simply to appear better for consumers. Green labels with leaves and the use of non-enforceable terms like "pure," "natural," or "clean" are a few obvious examples.

The term "organic," however, is trustworthy because you have to have the official certification in order to put it on your products.

That doesn't mean you have to deliberately look for the bad in every discovery, just look for the whole story. Environmental choices are best made with knowledge, not emotional whims.

Appendix

"5 Things To Buy In Bulk to Save Money + Reduce Waste." Change Your State. North Carolina State University, Mar. 2014.
http://sustainability.ncsu.edu/changeyourstate/5-things-buy-in-bulk-save-money/

"Fact Sheet: The Economic Challenge Posed by Declining Pollinator Populations." The White House. The White House, June 2014.
http://www.whitehouse.gov/the-press-office/2014/06/20/fact-sheet-economic-challenge-posed-declining-pollinator-populations

"U.S. Energy Information Administration - EIA - Independent Statistics and Analysis." How Much Electricity Does an American Home Use? U.S. Energy Information Administration, Jan. 2014.
http://www.eia.gov/tools/faqs/faq.cfm?id=97&t=3

"Paper Information." World Centric: Zero Waste Solutions. World Centric, 2014.
http://worldcentric.org/biocompostables/paper-info

Goldschein, Eric. "15 Outrageous Facts About The Bottled Water Industry." Business Insider. Business Insider, Inc, 27 Oct. 2011.
http://www.businessinsider.com/facts-bottled-water-industry-2011-10?op=1

"Bottled Water and Energy Fact Sheet." Pacific Institute: Research for People and the Planet. Pacific Institute, 2007.
http://pacinst.org/publication/bottled-water-and-energy-a-fact-sheet/

"10 Fast Facts on Recycling." Environmental Protection Agency. Environmental Protection Agency, n.d.
http://www.epa.gov/reg3wcmd/solidwasterecyclingfacts.htm

"How School Food Affects the Environment." Upload Knowledge. Center for Environmental Education, 2008.
http://www.ceeonline.org/greenGuide/food/upload/environmenthealth.aspx

"Recycling Stats." GreenWaste: A Brighter Shade of Green. GreenWaste, 2014.
http://www.greenwaste.com/recycling-stats

Kelly, Margie. "Top 7 Genetically Modified Crops." The Huffington Post. TheHuffingtonPost.com, 30 Oct. 2012
http://www.huffingtonpost.com/margie-kelly/genetically-modified-food_b_2039455.html

"What Is GMO? Agricultural Crops That Have a Risk of Being GMO." The Non GMO Project. The Non GMO Project, 2012
http://www.nongmoproject.org/learn-more/

Powers, Jenny. "NRDC Lauds Passage of New York City Council Legislation Requiring Groceries, Retailers to Provide Plastic Bag Recycling for Consumers." NRDC: Press Release. Natural Resources Defense Council, 9 Jan. 2008.
http://www.nrdc.org/media/2008/080109.asp

"Plastic Bags: Which Do You Choose--paper or Plastic?" Massachusetts Chapter Sierra Club. Sierra Club, 2014.
http://www.sierraclubmass.org/issues/conservation/plasticbags/plasticbags.html

Clark, Duncan, and Mike Berners-Lee. "What's the Carbon Footprint of ... a Load of Laundry?" Green Living Blog. The Guardian, 25 Nov. 2010 http://www.theguardian.com/environment/green-living-blog/2010/nov/25/carbon-footprint-load-laundry

"Rechargeable Battery Life Questions and Answers." Battery Savers. BatterySavers.com, 2014. http://www.batterysavers.com/Compare-Batteries-Questions.html

"The Environment." Sustainable Cycles. SustainableCycles.ca, 2014. http://sustainablecycles.ca/why-reusable/the-environment/

Boyer, Mark. "IKEA Consumes a Full One Percent of the World's Commercial Wood Supply." Inhabitat: Design Will Save the World. Inhabitat.com, 8 July 2013. http://inhabitat.com/one-percent-of-all-the-worlds-commercial-wood-is-used-to-make-ikea-products/

"My Jeans Are Very Thirsty!" It's Our Environment. Environmental Protection Agency, June 2010. http://blog.epa.gov/blog/2010/06/my-jeans-are-very-thirsty/

"Electronics Donation and Recycling." EPA ECycling. Environmental Protection Agency, 2014. http://www.epa.gov/epawaste/conserve/materials/ecycling/donate.htm

"The E-Waste Crisis Introduction." EStewards. EStewards.org, 2010. http://www.e-stewards.org/the-e-waste-crisis/

"Attention Drivers! Turn off Your Idling Engines." Environmental Defense Fund. EDF. org, 2014. http://www.edf.org/transportation/reports/idling

"How Much Water Do You Really Use? Do You Use Water Effectively?" FreeDrinking-Water.com. Free Drinking Water, n.d. http://www.freedrinkingwater.com/water_quality/common-daily-water-usage.htm

"Rainwater Harvesting." Http://rainwaterharvesting.tamu.edu. Texas A&M University, n.d. http://rainwaterharvesting.tamu.edu/catchment-area/

"How School Food Affects the Environment." Upload Knowledge. Center for Environmental Education, 2008. http://www.ceeonline.org/greenGuide/food/upload/environmenthealth.aspx

"U.S. Energy Information Administration - EIA - Independent Statistics and Analysis." How Much Carbon Dioxide Is Produced by Burning Gasoline and Diesel Fuel? U.S. Energy Information Administration, 21 May 2014. http://www.eia.gov/tools/faqs/faq.cfm?id=307&t=11

"Frequently Asked Questions: Holiday Waste Prevention." Stanford: Land, Buildings, and Real Estate. Stanford University, 2014. http://bgm.stanford.edu/pssi_faq_holiday_waste

"Plastics, Common Wastes & Materials." EPA.gov. Environmental Protection Agency, Feb. 2014.
http://www.epa.gov/osw/conserve/materials/plastics.htm

Wolford, Becca. "Hemp – One Of The Most Healthy Recyclable Substances Around." Wakingtimes.com. Waking Times, 12 Jan. 2013.
http://www.wakingtimes.com/2013/01/12/hemp-one-of-the-most-healthy-recyclable-substances-around/

Dunn, Collin. "Built In Dishwashers vs. Hand Washing: Which Is Greener?" TreeHugger.com. Tree Hugger, 22 Jan. 2009.
http://www.treehugger.com/kitchen-design/built-in-dishwashers-vs-hand-washing-which-is-greener.html

"LED Lights vs. Incandescent Light Bulbs vs. CFLs." Design Recycle Inc. N.p., 2014. Web.
http://www.designrecycleinc.com/led%20comp%20chart.html

"Disposable Lunch Facts - Items Carried in Work and School Lunches." Www.reuseit. com. Reuse It, 2010. Web.
http://www.reuseit.com/facts-and-myths/disposable-lunch-facts-items-carried-in-work-and-school-lunches.htm

"Plastic Straw Facts." Simply Straws. N.p., 2014. Web.
http://simplystraws.com/plastic-facts

"Junk Mail Impact: Stop the Nuisance & Environmental Hazard." 41pounds.org. 41 Pounds, 2014. Web.
https://www.41pounds.org/impact/

"Environmental Benefits: Reuse & Recycling Ink and Toner Cartridges." A Greener Refill. N.p., 2009. Web.
http://www.agreenerrefill.com/The-Benefits-of-Recycling

"How Much Electricity Does an American Home Use?" EIA - Independent Statistics and Analysis. U.S. Energy Information Administration, Jan. 2014. Web.
http://www.eia.gov/tools/faqs/faq.cfm?id=97&t=3

Gardella, Fiorella. "The Meat Industry....Is It worth It?" Seminar in Global Sustainability. University of California, Irvine, 2009. Web.
http://darwin.bio.uci.edu/sustain/global/sensem/MeatIndustry.html

"Go Vegetarian One Day a Week." Wanna Veg. N.p., 2014. Web.
http://wannaveg.com/

Ketler, Alanna. "Factory Farming Is Destroying Our Environment." Collective Evolution. N.p., 4 Mar. 2014. Web.
http://www.collective-evolution.com/2013/03/04/eating-meat-destruction-of-environment/

"Indoor Water Use in the United States." Water Sense. Environmental Protection Agency, July 2014. Web.
http://www.epa.gov/WaterSense/pubs/indoor.html

Poynter, Dan. "Book Industry Statistics." Dan Poynter's Para Publishing. Para Publishing, 2008. Web.
http://bookstatistics.com/sites/para/resources/statistics.cfm

"Food Waste Basics." Resource Conservation. United States Environmental Protection Agency, Mar. 2014. Web.
http://www.epa.gov/foodrecovery/

"Shade Grown Coffee: Organic, Fair Trade, Bird Friendly Coffee." Earth Easy, 2012. Web.
http://eartheasy.com/eat_shadegrown_coffee.htm

"Residential Heating Oil Prices -- What Consumers Should Know." Cornell Cooperative Extension. Tompkins County, 2003. Web.
http://ccetompkins.org/resources/residential-heating-oil-prices-what-consumers-should-know

"U.S. Outdoor Water Use." Water Sense. Environmental Protection Agency, Jan. 2014. Web.
http://www.epa.gov/WaterSense/pubs/outdoor.html

"Cotton: A Water Wasting Crop." Cotton Farming. World Wildlife Foundation, 2003. Web.
http://wwf.panda.org/about_our_earth/about_freshwater/freshwater_problems/thirsty_crops/cotton

"Reducing Waste in the Workplace." Reduce.org. Minnesota Pollution Control Agency, 2014. Web.
http://reduce.org/workplace/

Greenemeier, Larry. "Leaving PCs on Overnight Wastes Billions in Energy Costs, Study Says." Scientific American. N.p., Mar. 2009. Web.
http://www.scientificamerican.com/blog/post/leaving-pcs-on-overnight-wastes-bil-2009-03-30/?id=leaving-pcs-on-overnight-wastes-bil-2009-03-30

"Cigarette Butts Are Toxic Waste." Tobacco Free CA, 2010. Web.
http://www.tobaccofreeca.com/smoking-problem/impact/environment/

"Tobacco Information - Environment." Leave The Pack Behind. N.p., 2008. Web.
http://www.leavethepackbehind.org/tob environment.php

"Resource Conservation and Recovery Act." (n.d.): n. pag. SuperFund. U.S. Environmental Protection Agency, 2014. Web.
http://www.epa.gov/superfund/students/clas_act/haz-ed/ff06.pdf

Copeland, Larry. "Americans' Commutes Aren't Getting Longer." USA Today. Gannett, 05 Mar. 2013. Web.
http://www.usatoday.com/story/news/nation/2013/03/05/americans-commutes-not-getting-longer/1963409/

"How Much Carbon Dioxide Is Produced by Burning Gasoline and Diesel Fuel?" FAQs. U.S. Energy Information Administration, Apr. 2014. Web.
http://www.eia.gov/tools/faqs/faq.cfm?id=307&t=11

"Going Green: Downloading Music Is Good for the Environment." The American Consumer Institute. N.p., July 2008. Web. http://www.theamericanconsumer.org/2008/07/going-green-downloading-music-is-good-for-the-environment/

"How Do Electronic Payments Benefit the Environment?" FAQs. Pay It Green, 2006. Web. https://www.payitgreen.org/consumer/faq

"Standby Power Statistics." Lawrence Berkeley National Laboratory. U.S. Department of Energy, 2014. Web. http:// http://standby.lbl.gov

"An Introduction to Indoor Air Quality." Indoor Air. U.S. Environmental Protection Agency, 2012. Web. http://www.epa.gov/iaq/voc.html

"Drugs in the Water." Harvard Health Publications, June 2011. Web. http://www.health.harvard.edu/newsletters/Harvard_Health_Letter/2011/June/drugs-in-the-water

"R.E.D. Facts: DEET." R.E.D. Facts: DEET (n.d.): n. pag. Office of Prevention, Pesticides and Toxic Substances. U.S. Environmental Protection Agency, 2014. Web. http://www.epa.gov/oppsrrd1/REDs/factsheets/0002fact.pdf

"Wasted: How America Is Losing Up to 40 Percent of Its Food from Farm to Fork to Landfill." Food and Agriculture. National Resources Defense Council, 2014. Web. http://www.nrdc.org/food/wasted-food.asp

PUBLISHER'S NOTE:

Hugo Villabona

First off, we would like to thank Terri Paajanen for her enlightening and delightful spin on the project. To the three non for profit organizations: the Environmental Defense Fund, the Nature Conservancy and the Story of Stuff project, thank you for providing added outlets to continue the process of living green. You can learn more about the tremendous work they are doing by logging onto their websites or in the 52 Simple Ways to Live Green application (available on iTunes, Google Play and the Windows Store).

CPSIA information can be obtained at www.ICGtesting.com
Printed in the USA
BVOW10s2220090315

390720BV00006B/11/P